Marketing
Your Church
to the
Community

Abingdon Press & The Church of the Resurrection
Ministry Guides

Marketing Your Church to the Community

Peter Metz
Adam Hamilton, Series Editor

ABINGDON PRESS
Nashville

MARKETING YOUR CHURCH TO THE COMMUNITY

Copyright © 2007 by Abingdon Press

This book is printed on acid-free paper.

Library of Congress Cataloging-in-Publication Data

Metz, Peter, 1951- Marketing your church to the community / Peter Metz.
    p. cm. – (Ministry guides ; 9)
 ISBN-13: 978-0-687-33508-4 (binding: adhesive perfect/pbk. : alk. paper)
 1. Church marketing. I. Title.

 BV652.23.M48 2007
 254'.4–dc22

              2006033515

07 08 09 10 11 12 13 14 15 16—10 9 8 7 6 5 4 3 2 1
MANUFACTURED IN THE UNITED STATES OF AMERICA

Contents

FOREWORD

Perhaps you have a new church that is small, but growing and looking to take its weekly worship attendance to the next level. Or, you have an older church that's not growing as you think it could be or should be. Both of these situations share something in common. You know there are plenty of people in your community who are not attending church. People who could fill your worship services every weekend—if only you could get them in the front door. People in need of what you have to offer. People you want to attract, not just to fill the seats in your sanctuary, but because you feel you have something they need.

Today, churches are discovering that it isn't enough to offer energizing, uplifting worship services and dynamic ministry programs that sustain and support those looking to grow in their faith. Churches are learning that they also must be successful marketers if they hope to attract those in their community who aren't connected with a church but would benefit from what a church can bring to their lives.

Using his extensive experience in both secular and church marketing, Peter Metz gives readers easily accessible, practical information in this Abingdon Press & The Church of the Resurrection *Marketing Your Church to the Community* guide. It holds clear-cut information and thought-provoking ideas to help both layperson and professional get the word out that your church can make a difference in people's lives.

．．．．．．．．．．．．．．．．．．．．．．．．．．．．．．．．．．

At The Church of the Resurrection, we live daily with the goal to help people become deeply committed Christians. More than nominally religious. More than the Sunday pew holder. More than the spectator. We know these same people become more by doing more. We begin with the knowledge that people want the church to be theirs. They want to know God has a place for them. With that in mind, we recognized from the very start that specialized ministries utilizing the skills and talents of laypeople are fundamental to church life.

A church on the move will have specialized ministries capitalizing on the skills and talents of laypeople. They are your keys to succeed.

In developing these guides, we listened to the requests of smaller churches for practical resources to enlist laypeople for this purpose. These economical guides, written by proven leaders at our church, will serve as essential resources for innovative, creative, and, more than likely, nontraditional church workers who have little or no budget to work with. With these guides in hand, your laypeople will be ready to plunge into the work with excitement and courage instead of tentatively approaching it on tiptoe.

At the core of these guides is the belief that anything is possible. It's a challenge, but it's a truth. God can and does use us all—with that conviction we bring hope to the world.

Adam Hamilton
Senior Pastor
The Church of the Resurrection
Leawood, Kansas

Introduction

> AND HOW ARE THEY TO BELIEVE IN ONE OF WHOM THEY HAVE
> NEVER HEARD? AND HOW ARE THEY TO HEAR WITHOUT
> SOMEONE TO PROCLAIM HIM?—ROMANS 10:14

There was a time when church marketing was considered a little crass, a little too "commercial." Of course, businesses had marketing plans designed to improve their bottom line. But churches were above that. Well, welcome to the twenty-first century. A look at the most successful churches today will confirm that marketing and advertising are frequently contributing to their success.

So what exactly do we mean by marketing and, by extension, advertising—marketing's most visible component? For answers to this, let's break it down to its simplest form. Let's go back to the 1700s. Let's assume there is a new baker in your town who has just opened his new shop on Main Street. What is the first thing he does? He hangs a sign out in front of the shop to let people know that there is a bakery inside.

If he is smart, the sign will be professional looking and designed to be friendly and inviting. That's marketing. He's letting the people walking by know what type of business he has (a bakery) and what type of shopping experience people might find inside (professional, yet friendly). If he is a little more aggressive, he may pass out handbills on the street corners that extol the virtues of his bakery and list the kinds of baked goods he has available.

Now, marketing has come a long way from simple signs and handbills, but the principles haven't really changed from what that baker might have done. The goal of marketing has always been to reach potential customers with a message that will entice them to consider doing business with you. *When it comes to churches, the goal is to make people in the community aware of what the church is like, what the church has to offer, and how they can benefit from that offering.*

That sounds simple enough, but it's not. People these days are frequently on overload. They have too many demands on their time and too many businesses and organizations trying to get their attention. So they tend to block out most of the messages sent in their direction. Yet that doesn't mean that churches shouldn't try. In fact, I believe that churches have a responsibility to reach out to the unchurched in their community, proclaim the good news of Jesus Christ and his resurrection, and help people find salvation.

So how do you reach these people and convince them to visit your worship service next weekend—or even next month? And do it with a limited budget because, as we all know, every church has a limited budget. This ministry guide will provide some answers to this all-important question and offer some ideas on what you can do even if you don't know much about marketing and have only a shoestring budget.

While on the surface this ministry guide may look like it's about growing your worship attendance, really that's not the case. Certainly, you will see some strategies and ideas that can help you do that. But, this guide is really about something much more important than that.

I hope you will discover that this guide is about reaching out to those in your community who don't have a church family, perhaps are nonbelievers, and introducing them to Jesus Christ and helping them begin a faith walk that will change their lives forever. Doing this is not only important, it is what we are being called to do. To paraphrase Paul in Romans 10, people need to hear the good news of the gospel before they can believe it, and we are being called to proclaim that good news.

CHAPTER ONE

Getting the Message Right

Have you ever gone to a restaurant that you knew nothing about other than the fact that it was a restaurant? Probably not. Before going to a restaurant to eat, you would likely want to know what the cuisine is—French, American, Italian, seafood, pizza, or burgers; maybe what the price range is; whether it is a good place for kids or something about its reputation.

Consider your options.

Restaurant A is, well, a restaurant and that's all you know about it.

Restaurant B is a casual, family-friendly place that serves burgers, steaks, and seafood, but is particularly proud of its pasta dishes. This restaurant is moderately priced and has been in business at the same location since 1951.

Now, you might not be interested in Restaurant B because what you really have a taste for is Mexican food. Or perhaps you are planning an anniversary dinner and the last thing you want is a bunch of kids at the next table. But at least you'll know before making the mistake of showing up at Restaurant B's door. And, if you do have kids, Restaurant B could be perfect for what you have in mind—less expense and more variety. On the other hand, you may never even consider Restaurant A simply because you don't know anything about it.

So what does all this have to do with churches? If people know nothing more about your church other than the fact that it is a church, visitors aren't likely to show up at your door. If you are hoping to have a steady stream of new people showing up on Sunday morning, it only makes sense that you'll be more successful if people know in advance what is important to you and what they can expect from your worship service.

Yes, we are talking about building awareness for your church, and if you aren't making a concerted effort to do this, you are either so well-known in your community that you don't need to tell people who you are or you are missing an opportunity to connect with people, create a growing, vibrant church, and help those in your community who don't attend church to find a place where they can begin their journey of faith.

By now you may be thinking, "Oh, no. Newspapers, radio, television. It takes a lot of money to advertise!" However, building awareness is nothing more than helping people understand who you are. And, there are opportunities to reach people with your message no matter what your budget. But before we get to those options, you need to consider what your message is going to be. What is it that you want people to know about your church that is likely to make them want to visit?

This chapter is designed to help you think through this important question because it costs no more to get the message right, and getting it wrong can be expensive in terms of wasted dollars, wasted time, and wasted effort. However, before you can start thinking about the message, you need to wrestle with defining who you are as a church and then what types of people will most likely be attracted to you.

Defining Who You Are

When professional product marketers set out to develop an advertising campaign, they start by fully understanding their product. For marketers, it's not enough to know what their product is. They want to know what their product does or doesn't do, what it does well and doesn't do well, what makes it unique or special, why people buy it, where they buy it, how they use it, and what they do when they don't have it. Just as marketers need to know their product, churches need to do the same. Your church must go through the hard work of defining its place and its role.

Why do people attend your church and what keeps them coming back? Is it the senior pastor? The children's or youth programs? Your tenets as a church? Your friendly atmosphere and your members? Your service times and location? Learn what people like and dislike (be honest) about your church, how people would describe it, and where your church fits into your community's landscape.

How do product marketers get answers to their questions? They do consumer research. They might do quantitative surveys involving hundreds—even thousands—of people. Or, focus groups where they will bring in eight to ten people as a group and ask them to talk about their product. Or, they might do one-on-ones, in which they bring people in one at a time to ask them questions. If these things work for marketers, why not use them for your church? The church embodies the most-needed product, so why not use the best means available to get its message disseminated?

I'm not suggesting that you need to survey hundreds of people. But, you can survey your members and visitors in person, by mail, by e-mail, or by a questionnaire inserted in your worship bulletin. You can hold a forum with your church council or board of elders. You can ask your staff for their views—they usually have a pretty good feel for what makes your church tick. Or, better still, you can do a combination of these things and get a broader cross section of opinion.

Positioning Statement (Mission Statement)

Ultimately, you want to take all of the information that you have gathered and use it to create what marketers call a **Positioning Statement.** You may prefer to call it a **Mission Statement**. A mission statement is a clear articulation of who you are, what is important to you, and where you are going as a church. It is a statement that all parts of the church—pastors, staff, members—understand and agree with. This is because everything that the church does should support the church's mission. I'd be surprised if you haven't already done some of this and have a pretty good idea why people are worshiping with you.

At The Church of the Resurrection, our mission statement is as follows:

> To build a Christian community where non-religious and nominally religious people are becoming deeply committed Christians.

In Darien, Illinois there is a church of slightly over a hundred members with a focus of building bridges to the urban community, so they define their mission specifically:

> We are a ministry seeking to present the age-old truths of Christianity in a culturally relevant way, especially as they relate to people who have given up on church and/or God.

In both cases, you can pretty quickly understand what is important to each church and what it is trying to be.

Importantly, each statement also defines how the church wants to present itself *from a marketing perspective.*

However, your mission statement is not necessarily the message you want to communicate to those who don't know you. Typically, a mission statement will be too long, sometimes a little dry, and it may not be the first thing that you would want to tell someone about your church. For example, I believe that **"To build a Christian community where non-religious and nominally religious people are becoming deeply committed Christians"** is a wonderful expression of who we are at The Church of the Resurrection and what we are trying to be. It's been the focus of everything that we have done at Resurrection since day one. However, it is a pretty complicated idea to share with someone who doesn't know our church. I wouldn't want to write a print ad that tried to communicate that thought and suspect that, if we did, the ad would be less than memorable.

Your mission statement also may not factor in an important part of message creation—defining whom you want to reach with your message. However, your message should spring from your mission statement and reflect it. I'll offer a suggestion on how to make that happen shortly, but first, if you don't have a mission statement, spend the time to develop one. You won't regret it. It will help you focus on what you are trying to accomplish as a church, and it will become a measuring stick for all that you do.

Next, with your mission statement in hand I'd ask that you consider whom you want to reach.

Identifying Whom You Want to Reach

There are two important reasons for having a description of those in your community that you think you have the best opportunity to attract with your message. First, while it would be ideal to talk to everyone in your community, doing that is probably not practical or affordable. Instead, you want to place your efforts toward those you stand the best chance of attracting. Second, by knowing who your best prospects are, you can tailor your message—or speak more directly—to those people.

Marketers define in detail the people they want to reach to ensure that their message is not only reaching the right people but also is delivering the most compelling message for that group in the right language and the right tone. For example, when Kellogg's advertises Froot Loops®, the company wants to talk to kids about the cereal's great taste and how much fun it is to eat using language that kids will respond to. Call it "kid speak." But if the company is advertising Special K®, it wants to talk to women about nutrition and how the cereal can be part of a healthy diet. The advertising would not use kid jargon. Seems pretty obvious, doesn't it?

Target Definition

So, how do you define your target audience? Marketers start by defining their target **demographically**. This could include hard information like age, income, occupation, marital status, and residence. However, marketers go beyond this and define their target **psychographically**. That is, they want to get inside their target's head and know what is important to him or her and what the attitudes are when it comes to the company's product.

Marketers frequently use their current customers as the best indicators of what their target looks like and what is on their minds. You can do the same. In fact, you probably already know the demographics of your congregation. And, from the research you did in developing your mission statement, you should also already know how your congregation feels about the church, what these people value in a church, whether they attended church in the past, and what it is about your church that attracted them. You need this information when you begin to craft your message.

At The Church of the Resurrection, we define our target as being:

> People who live within easy driving distance from the church. They are likely to be in the 30 to 50 age group and could be single, married, or married with children. They currently don't attend church and may have little or no faith. However, they feel something is missing in their lives and think that maybe going to church would be a good thing. But they can't explain why. Therefore, going to church hasn't been a priority for them.

This target definition provides some hard information about age, marital status, and geography. But more importantly, it tells us something about where our target is in relation to church and faith. This definition becomes critical information for creating a message that talks to them in ways that they will respond to.

Articulating Your Message

Now comes the tough part. Armed with a good understanding of who you are and want to be—your mission statement—and a good sense for whom you want to reach—your target audience—you are ready to develop your message. Marketers would call this their **Selling Proposition**, but **Message** sounds a little more "church-like."

One main idea

There are, no doubt, so many things you would like to tell a potential visitor about your church that the temptation is to try to tell them everything in the hopes that something will hit a responsive chord. To avoid this temptation, marketers will focus on the ONE MAIN IDEA that they think is the most compelling reason someone should buy their product. It's the one net impression that they would like their target to take away from their advertising. This doesn't mean that you can only tell your target one thing. In fact, you may want to give them a bunch of information about your church. And that can be okay. But, and this is a big BUT, everything that you tell them should support the ONE MAIN IDEA. (If you sense that I think this one main idea thing is important, it is.)

To help in identifying that one main idea, marketers will write a **Creative Strategy**. Another way of saying it is **Message Strategy**. Creative strategies come in many forms, but the one that I have had the greatest success with begins with a statement describing the target's current mind-set and behavior as a result of that mind-set. These are both based on the **target definition**. It finishes with what you would like the target to believe about you and the action you would like to have the target take based on that desired belief. Your message is what will move the target from the current belief to the desired belief.

MESSAGE STRATEGY

Current
Belief
The target's
current
mind-set.

Message
What you
want to
communicate.

Desired Belief
What you
would like
the target
to believe.

Current Action
What the
target does
based on
current belief.

Desired Action
What you
would like the
target to do
in the future.

The purpose for going through this exercise is that it forces you to really think about the people you want to reach out to and attract and then identify the main reason you can give them for considering your church.

At The Church of the Resurrection, our message strategy looks like this.

<u>Current Belief</u>
Going to church would probably be a good idea, but it's not important to me.

<u>Message</u>
The Church of the Resurrection is a place that is making a difference in people's lives.

<u>Desired Belief</u>
The Church of the Resurrection is a place that can make a difference in my life.

<u>Current Action</u>
Rarely, if ever, goes to church except for Christmas and Easter.

<u>Desired Action</u>
Visits The Church of the Resurrection for worship to see what it is like.

The message is our ONE MAIN IDEA.

Supporting the Message

There is one more piece to this exercise. Remember when I said that you could include a bunch of information as long as it all supported the one main idea or message? We call this information *our support* for why the message is believable. The idea is that if you can't support the claim in your message, it won't be believable. At Resurrection, we believe there are a number of reasons we can make a difference in people's lives:

- Relevant sermons.
- Passionate worship.
- Opportunities to learn more about Christianity.
- Opportunities to meet others like me.
- Opportunities to give back to my community and help others.

I would like to think that the Resurrection message strategy is unique to The Church of the Resurrection and that if a hundred churches all wrote their own message strategy, no two strategies would be the same. This is because the message strategy should be a reflection of each church's mission statement and target audience—a reflection of what makes each church unique.

I can almost guarantee that if you take the time to thoughtfully craft your **mission statement**, your **target definition,** and your **message strategy**, your communications efforts will be more focused, do a better job of presenting who you are as a church, and talk more directly to the people whom you have the best opportunity to attract.

One way to think about the message strategy is simply that it is the public face you want to present to people. It is how you want people to view you. At The Church of the Resurrection, we want people to see us as a church that is making a difference in people's lives. Given this, we want all of our external communications or contacts with people to be consistent with our message strategy.

All of our communications should be measured against the strategy to make sure that we are communicating the right message. If the goal is to plant one single-minded idea in people's minds about who you are, it only follows that the more consistently you deliver that idea, the more successful you will be in communicating it. With every communication, whether it is a media-delivered ad or commercial, a mail piece, your website, or even flyers and posters, you should ask yourself, *Does this deliver our message? Does it communicate how we want people to think about our church?*

Armed with the right message strategy, you will eventually even want to consider it when planning programs or events. Even your worship service should reflect the core idea of your strategy. Now, I'm not suggesting that your worship service should be turned into one long communications piece, but it should be a reflection of how you want people to think about your church.

But, let's take it one step at a time. Once you have figured out what it is that you want to communicate to people, you need to determine the best way to reach people with that message. Before you can begin writing and designing your communications, you will need to decide on what form those communications will take. Is it a print ad, a radio commercial, a poster, or a mail piece?

Selecting Options for Reaching Your Target Group

Once you have developed your message strategy defining whom you want to reach and what you want to communicate to them, it's time to figure out the best way to reach them. I wish that I could just tell you the best way to reach your target. However, after twenty-five years in the advertising agency business helping large national companies figure out how best to reach their targets, I know that no two situations are alike. What works for one church may not work for another, and parts of media selection are somewhat subjective.

Let's go back to our restaurant analogy. If you are a family-style restaurant serving great burgers and pizza, you want to reach families with kids at home. To do this, you may run ads in the local newspaper and maybe ads in the high school football program telling parents and kids to come on over after the game. But if you are an upscale steak house, you are better served running ads in the local style and fashion magazine and doing mailings to the homes in your community's more affluent neighborhoods. These are two restaurants with different offerings, wanting to reach different target audiences, and employing different strategies for success. Likewise, different churches will have different strategies.

Considerations

Before we get to the options, let's frame our discussion based on things to consider when deciding which option or options is right for you. Among those considerations are your target, your budget, your message, and what we might call your level of creative sophistication. By that I mean if you don't think you can create and produce a television commercial, you are probably better off eliminating TV from your list of options.

Your target

Understanding your target becomes critical so you are using media that efficiently reach your intended audience and so you aren't reaching a lot of people whom it doesn't make sense to reach. For example, I started out as a media buyer on an airlines account. I was responsible for their trade and special interest budgets. One of our targets was funeral directors. Believe it or not, a lot of bodies get shipped by air because when people die out of town, there aren't a lot of options for getting them home. Now, we may have been able to reach every funeral director in the country through *Time* magazine or *Sports Illustrated*. But, we would have also reached a lot of people who weren't funeral directors and buying ads in those magazines would have cost a lot of money. So instead, we placed our ads in a trade magazine called *Mortuary Management* that efficiently zeroed in on the funeral-director market.

Let's assume for the moment that you want to reach people who live in fairly close proximity to your church, and you are considering television or radio. These are both media that typically cover a large geographic area, so if you use them, you may be spending money to reach a lot of people who really aren't part of your target group. The local newspaper or a mail campaign targeting your local neighborhoods may be better ideas.

Or, let's say that you want to reach younger adults. Statistics show they are not very big on reading the newspaper, so newspaper ads may not make sense. Also, younger adults move frequently, so buying a good mailing list may be difficult since many of the addresses on the list could be out-of-date. But young adults do listen to a lot of radio, so perhaps buying time on a local rock station is the right choice.

One more example. Assume you want to reach people who don't go to church and have at best a minimal level of faith. These are folks who probably don't listen to Christian radio or read Christian publications, so don't spend your money there. But they do go to the movies frequently, so maybe running ads in the lead-in to movies at the local theater makes sense. You get the picture. You need to consider your target's habits when deciding how to reach them.

Your budget

How much you can spend is clearly going to be a factor in deciding what you are going to do. If you have ever bought a house, you know that the first thing you have to decide is how much you are willing to pay. Then you look at houses only in your price range. Otherwise, you can spend a lot of time looking at houses you can't afford—or worse, find a house that you really want to buy, but can't afford.

Just as home buyers do, marketers will start by setting a budget so that they don't consider things they can't afford. They will also think about how expensive something is based on two considerations.

▷ **Total** Cost of Option. First, what is the total cost of an option? Airing radio commercials isn't very expensive individually, but you have to run a number of them to effectively communicate with your target. If you can't afford to run a number of radio commercials, scratch radio off your list. If you think television is a good idea, be sure to factor in the cost of producing a commercial into the total cost of a TV campaign.

▷ **Efficiency** of Option. Second, is the option efficient in reaching the target? Marketers will look at options on a "cost per thousand" basis, so they can determine which options reach their target in the most cost efficient way. The lower the cost per thousand is, the more cost effective the option. However, it's not as simple as that. If it were, people would simply run small space newspaper ads that would have a low cost per thousand. And they would never do a mail piece because mail has a much higher cost per thousand. But, a mailer may actually be more efficient if you are trying to reach a small geographic area because you can limit your mailing to that area. And, it may be a more effective way to communicate your message than a small newspaper ad because it will have more space to communicate. Did I mention that this can all become somewhat subjective?

Your message

Some media options are better at delivering certain types of communications than others. For example, if you want to make sure people can capture your location, phone number, or website address, print may be better than TV or billboards. Did you ever try to remember a phone number that was in a radio or television commercial? It's tough to do no matter how many times they repeat it. So, if having people remember your phone number is critical to your communication, you are better off with something printed. But, if you want to let people know how moving or dynamic your worship service is, you may conclude that you can communicate that better with television, where you can use sight and sound. You have to ask yourself, *Does my message fit the medium?*

Your level of creative sophistication

I have a passion for golf. Over time, I have learned that while I love to play golf, I'm never going to be very good at it. I've also learned that there are golf shots that I can make and there are golf shots that I can't. When I try the shots I can't make, I usually get myself in trouble. Let's say my ball ends up behind a tree. The right shot would be to draw the ball so that it goes around the tree and comes out safely on the other side. But I can't make that shot, would probably hit the tree and end up with my ball in some worse place. So instead, I will chip the ball sideways out from behind the tree to a place where I can hit it safely. Just as my success in golf is predicated on knowing what I can and cannot do, yours in developing successful communications may depend on what you think you can do.

POTENTIAL PITFALL

For some, the idea of creating a television commercial is overwhelming. If that's the case, don't try to use television. If it is easier for you to create a newspaper ad or a mail piece, stick to what you think you can do well. It is better to do a newspaper ad well than a television commercial poorly. Remember every time you communicate with someone, it says something about who you are. A poorly done television commercial may say that you aren't very professional, don't know what you are doing, or don't have very high standards. I think you'd agree that those aren't conclusions you'd like to have potential visitors make about your church.

Options

Armed with these four considerations, it's time to consider some of your options. Following is how I would suggest that you think about a number of them. You may agree or disagree with my analysis based on your specific situation. And that's fine. The important thing is that you go through the thought process and use the four considerations in evaluating the options available to you.

Local newspapers

Local newspapers are popular. Many newspapers have a faith or religion section one day of the week (usually Saturday), and if people are church shopping, it's a good place to start. The newspaper can be an effective place to deliver your message. And, it's a good place to tell people where your church is located and how to reach it by phone or the Internet.

Depending on the market, you may have a large newspaper or you may have local newspapers for your town or county. The disadvantage of newspaper advertising is that the production quality isn't very good. The ads are usually black and white, and the reproduction of pictures is not always good. But, if newspaper reproduction is good enough for your message and if you have a newspaper that reaches your geographic target, newspaper may be a good option. At The Church of the Resurrection, we use newspaper advertising to communicate our message to people who are turning to the newspaper ads to help them decide which churches they will visit.

Yellow pages

The yellow pages—a commonly used media for churches. If you want to make it easy for people to find your address and phone number, there may be no better place to do this than the yellow pages. As a result, it seems unlikely that a church wouldn't want to have a presence in the yellow pages.

The real question is how big a presence is right for you. At The Church of the Resurrection, we used to run fairly large ads in the Kansas City yellow pages. We wanted to stand out in the crowd. However, doing this was very expensive. Over time we came to realize that most people turning to the yellow pages have probably already heard of us. They have reached that stage in their "church shopping" where they simply want to know our address, or they want to be able to call us for directions and worship times. We don't need an ad to meet this need. Today, we have a bold one-inch listing, but no ad. This adjustment cut our yellow pages spending by over half. That savings became money that we could use more effectively elsewhere.

Radio

Radio can be effective if you have a very specific target in mind. If yours is like most markets, you have a lot of radio stations to choose from. You may have rock stations to reach young adults, "oldies" stations to reach baby boomers, sports stations to reach men, or news and talk stations to reach higher income and better educated people. You can even pick and choose specific programs on stations to better target those you want to reach.

However, you need to run a lot of commercials on radio to make an impression, and it may be difficult to communicate your address, phone number, or web address. Radio as a creative medium can also be a challenge. People will mentally tune out your message quickly if it isn't interesting and you have no visuals to get people's attention. Radio may also cover a much wider geographic area than you are interested in reaching.

Television

Television has become much more affordable with the advent of cable. I won't go into a dissertation on how cable has revolutionized the television industry, but it suffices to say that today programs have lower ratings because viewers have so many more choices—and lower ratings mean lower prices. You can even buy time from local cable providers that deliver viewers in smaller geographic areas. Both of these things have made running a television campaign more practical from a cost perspective. However, like radio, you can't just run a few commercials and assume that your message has gotten through to your target audience—because just a few commercials won't reach a large percentage of your target. You need to run a bunch of commercials over time, so TV can still be expensive.

POTENTIAL PITFALL

One major advantage of television is that it provides you with both sight and sound, making it a truly creative medium. On the negative side, if you lack expertise, it is easy to create a commercial that looks amateurish, and that can hurt you more than it helps you. So, be sure you can take advantage of the medium's strengths if you are considering going down that path.

Direct mail

Direct mail is an option that we use often at The Church of the Resurrection for its ability to target specific geographic areas. While the printing and postage can be somewhat pricey on a per-piece basis, we believe that our ability to produce a professional looking piece and deliver it directly to the homes around our church outweighs the cost.

Today, you can buy mailing lists targeting practically any group. At The Church of the Resurrection, we buy a list of the homes within a three-mile radius of the church and typically mail them large, oversized postcards. But, you don't have to limit your efforts to postcards. Letters, brochures, and flyers can also be effective, depending on your particular message. A mailing service, or possibly a printer, can help you buy the list and can handle sending the mailing out. It's one of the times we have found that the additional cost of such services can be outweighed by the postage savings the mailing service can provide by batching our mailings by zip code and postal route.

That said, some caution must be applied in buying lists. A general list is likely to be the most up-to-date. Very specific lists like one that only includes "head of household who is college educated with a professional or managerial occupation" will be more difficult for the list supplier to collect and, therefore, less likely to be as current. And, you don't want to waste your mailing dollars on lists that aren't as current as possible.

For our Young Adult Ministry, we once bought a list of adults ages eighteen to thirty living within a five-mile radius of our church to target the large number of apartment complexes in our area. But based on the poor response, we concluded that renters move so often that the list was probably not current enough.

Outdoor billboards

Outdoor billboards are tried by churches from time to time. The inclination is that you can't go wrong if you buy a billboard close to the church that has a lot of traffic driving past it. We have no experience with billboards, so I am hesitant to pass judgment on the idea, but keep in mind that just because people are passing the billboard doesn't mean that they are seeing your message or retaining much of it. Advertisers think of billboards as a reminder medium, simply reinforcing a message that is delivered in greater detail somewhere else. If you can afford this reminder strategy, billboards may make sense. But keep your billboard message very short and recognize the limitations of the medium.

Flyers and posters

Flyers and posters are probably the most commonly used communications forms that churches use because they are inexpensive and enable a church to support its smaller programs and ministries. You can also control distribution. Flyers can be available in your church narthex and passed out in targeted ways. Attach them to door knobs in your neighborhood, pass them out in high traffic retail areas, or even pass them out at children's sports events. Local retailers will sometimes put up a poster for churches. The important thing to remember, whether your flyer or poster is for an event or a ministry, is that it must reinforce your overall message strategy. Don't get off message just because it's a flyer. Use the flyer to both advertise the event and deliver your larger message.

Website

No discussion of communications is complete without some comment on **websites**. If you don't have one—get one quick. We have learned that our website is not only an effective and cost-efficient way of communicating with our own members but also it has become a significant tool in outreach. We are amazed how many people come to our website to learn information about our church and its worship services. Sometimes they have already heard about us and want to learn more. Sometimes they do searches trying to find a church in their local area. If they search "Churches, Leawood, Kansas," they will find us quite easily.

Our website also enables us to reduce the amount of information in our other forms of communications and more single-mindedly focus on our ONE MAIN IDEA. This is because we put our web address on all of our communications and direct people to our website for additional information. Fewer words, shorter pieces, and more focus on what's really important to communicate. You have to love that concept.

If you have followed chapter 1, you now have defined your message and identified the people to reach with it.

Chapter 2 has summarized the options. You can figure out the best ways of reaching those people by considering the target's habits, your budget limitations, and your message. Chapter 3 will discuss crafting your message for the media options you have selected.

CHAPTER THREE

What to Say and How to Say It

Your communications pieces, whether a newspaper ad, radio commercial, direct mail piece or website, should be uniquely tailored to who you are as a church and what your message strategy is. Theoretically at least, no two churches' ads, mailers, or websites should look or sound the same. So once again, I can't tell you what to do. All I can do is tell you how we at The Church of the Resurrection go about developing communications and hope that you will learn some things that you can apply to your own communications development. In other words, while the end results may be very different, the principles that lead to those results should by and large be the same.

As you will recall, at The Church of the Resurrection our message strategy is that *The Church of the Resurrection is a place that is making a difference in people's lives.* While that is what we want to communicate, it's not literally what we want to say. We have simplified this thought to three words. **Relevant. Passionate. Life-Changing**. I know, actually that is four words, but you get the idea. We believe that this set of words clearly articulates what we want to communicate to people. It's concise, it's simple, it's memorable, and it expresses how we think about ourselves and want others to think about us as well. Therefore, it is a set of words that you will see in almost all of our communications pieces.

Newspaper Ads

First question: how big should your newspaper ads be? Our philosophy is that we can't afford to run extremely large ads because we want to be in the newspapers every week. So, we have decided that while we are the biggest church in our area, we don't want to have an ad that is bigger than other churches. We simply want an ad that is big enough to deliver our message without breaking our budget. For us, that is an ad that is two columns by four inches or about a four-inch square.

While we have a whole laundry list of things we could tell people about Resurrection, we also know that one simple idea is much more likely to be absorbed by the reader. So this ad is headlined with our positioning line. **Relevant. Passionate. Life-Changing**. The copy is designed to reinforce our headline idea and while there is detailed information about service times and styles, this information is subservient to the main message: **Relevant, Passionate, Life-Changing**.

It's not hard to see what we think is important to communicate. Sure, we could tell people about our children's program or our Bible studies or our missions ministries. But we believe that if people find our simple message to be intriguing, they will go to our website to find out more or show up for a worship service to see what we are all about.

You will also notice that we have pictures of people at the top of the ad. They are there for three reasons.

Relevant
Messages

Passionate
Worship

Life-Changing
Ministries

If you're looking for a worship experience you will not soon forget, join us this weekend. Enjoy powerful contemporary music in our evening services or moving traditional music in our morning services, and a message that will encourage, inspire and send you home with hope.

Saturday & Sunday Evening 5:00 p.m.
Contemporary worship and music

Sunday Morning 7:45, 9:00, 10:45 a.m.*
Traditional worship and music
Childcare available at all services. *Interpreted for the Deaf
Special needs services available.

The United Methodist Church of the
RESURRECTION
13720 Roe Avenue, (between Roe and Nall on 137th)
Leawood, Kansas 66224, 913-897-0120, www.cor.org

1. They add visual interest to the ad.

2. Given that our message strategy is *The Church of the Resurrection is a place that is making a difference in people's lives,* showing people reinforces that message.

3. At Resurrection, we realize that our size is an issue for some people. In fact, we once mailed a piece with the headline "Why would anyone attend a church this big?" The people at the top of our ad subtly address this issue by saying that we are a church of individuals, not just a big church. I should also note that the people in the ad are from Resurrection. They aren't models or pictures we bought. We want our ads to be honest and real, and using "real people" helps us do that.

Specific sermon series

We also run ads that support specific sermon series. Not all sermon series, but those that we think will attract a non-religious or nominally religious person. When we do this, the focus of the ads is on the sermon series, but our hope is that people will consider the topic and conclude that not only is it interesting but also that this is a church delivering relevant messages that can make a difference in a person's life.

Do the latest scientific discoveries threaten the religious faith?

Or confirm it?

Join us for the provocative, new series of sermons, **Where Science and Religion Meet**. Rev. Adam Hamilton will interview scientists, review the leading scientific ideas and explore the latest scientific discoveries – all with an eye to understanding the relationship between science and the Christian faith.

Don't miss this exciting sermon series January 9 - February 13

Saturday & Sunday* Evening 5:00 p.m.
Contemporary worship and music

Sunday Morning 7:45, 9:00, 10:45 a.m.
Traditional worship and music

Childcare available at all services. *Interpreted for the Deaf

The United Methodist Church of the
Resurrection
13720 Roe Ave., (between Roe and Nall on 137th)
Leawood, KS 66224, 913-897-0120, www.cor.org

Holiday worship

As you might guess, holiday worship is a great opportunity to attract our target group to our doors. You will recall that our target's current action is that they "rarely, if ever, go to church except for Christmas and Easter." Well, if that is the best time to get them to sample what we have to offer, we want to be sure that they feel welcomed and know when we are holding services. So our holiday worship newspaper ads are designed to communicate those two things. Prior to one Christmas Eve, we asked ourselves, "With every church offering Christmas Eve worship, what makes Christmas Eve at Resurrection unique?" We concluded that it was that while most churches typically hold a candlelight service as their last service of the evening, at Resurrection every Christmas Eve service is a candlelight service. We thought that would be attractive to our target group—people whose best memories

Seven Candlelight services.

One glorious story.

Thursday, December 23	**Friday, December 24**			
6:30 pm Contemporary*	3:00 pm Children & Family*	7:00 pm	Chancel Choir* & Orchestra	
8:00 pm Contemporary* and Communion	Children Choir	8:30 pm	Chancel Choir* & Orchestra	
*Childcare for children 3 and under	5:00 pm Children & Family*†	11:00 pm	Youth Choir	
†Interpreted for the Deaf	Children Choir		and Communion	

The United Methodist Church of the
Resurrection
13720 Roe Avenue, (between Roe and Nall on 137th)
Leawood, Kansas 66224, 913-897-0120, www.cor.org

Celebrate the Joy of Easter!

Saturday, March 26
5:00 pm Contemporary Worship
7:00 pm Contemporary Worship

Sunday, March 27
7:30 am Traditional Worship
9:00 am Traditional Worship
11:00 am Traditional Worship*
5:00 pm Contemporary Worship

Worship will also be offered in our
Fellowship Hall at 9:15 am and 11:15 am

Childcare for children 3 and under available at all services.
Special needs services available. * Interpreted for the Deaf.

The United Methodist Church of the
Resurrection
13720 Roe Ave., (between Roe and Nall on 137th)
Leawood, KS 66224, 913-897-0120, www.cor.org

*As they entered the tomb, they saw a young man dressed in a white robe...
Don't be alarmed he said, You are looking for Jesus the Nazarene, who was crucified.*

HE IS RISEN

of Christmas Eve worship were probably of a candlelight service. So it became the focus for our ad: "Seven Candlelight Services. One Glorious Story."

For Easter, we again asked ourselves what made Easter worship a unique experience. We knew that Easter worship would be a joyous and moving experience for everyone attending, but we didn't seem to have a specific claim that we could focus on like we did at Christmas. So, we decided to simply underscore that Easter worship at Resurrection would be a service that focused on the good news of the resurrection: He Is Risen. In smaller print, we included details of times and style of worship.

Yellow Pages

As I mentioned, our philosophy on yellow pages advertising has changed over time. We used to run large ads that delivered a lot of what we thought was important information for someone looking for a church. But then we realized that what this ad was communicating was that we had a lot of stuff, but no one main idea was coming through the ads.

So, we adjusted to a smaller, less-expensive ad that actually was a variation of our first ad, but without listing specific worship times since worship times change. (You can only change your yellow pages ad once a year.)

That smaller ad was an improvement. However, ultimately we concluded that the most important thing to communicate in the yellow pages was our address, phone number, and web address. Today, we do this through a bold, two-color, one-inch listing. However, immediately after our name, The Church of the Resurrection, we still managed to sneak our **"Relevant. Passionate. Life-Changing."** line into our listing to provide some positioning.

```
┌─────────────────────────────────────────┐
│ THE CHURCH OF THE RESURRECTION           │
│                                          │
│ Relevant. Passionate. Life-Changing.     │
│ Traditional Worship:  Sunday morning     │
│ Contemporary Worship: Sat. and Sun. evenings │
│ 137th Street between Roe and Nall        │
│ For worship times:                       │
│ www.cor.org        913-897-0120          │
└─────────────────────────────────────────┘
```

Direct Mail

The official opening of our new 3,200-seat sanctuary occurred on an Easter weekend. We realized that it was likely that we could become known simply as that really big church at 137th Street and Roe Avenue. That is not how we wanted to be perceived, so to counteract that possible "really big church" perception, we mailed a series of postcards to the twenty thousand households in a three-mile radius of the church. The message of this campaign was, you guessed it, "The Church of the Resurrection is a place that is making a difference in people's lives." Each postcard featured an individual member of our church because we are a church of people, not buildings. In fact, we didn't even mention the new building. The headlines and copy communicated how we are making a difference in people's lives.

As you read before, we run newspaper advertising from time to time that focuses on sermon series that we believe will be particularly interesting to nonreligious and nominally religious people. For example, Senior Pastor Adam Hamilton delivered an eight-week series on how other denominations differ from us as United Methodists and what we could learn from the other denominations. Each week, we even included worship elements from the other denominations. It was a series that we thought visitors might find especially intriguing if they grew up in a denomination other than United Methodist. So, we sent out a postcard supporting the series.

Examples of the series of postcards mailed to twenty thousand households in a three-mile radius of The Church of the Resurrection. The message is, The Church of the Resurrection is a place that is making a difference in people's lives.

COR has ways to help.

If you want to make a difference in other's lives and in your own, then the Church of the Resurrection may be right for you.

- Join us every other Saturday morning for FaithWorks where hundreds of our members serve throughout the Kansas City area to make our city a better place.
- Help us build a house for Habitat for Humanity in Kansas City, Kansas. Our church has helped construct 70 homes in the last ten years.
- Join us in providing meals for thousands of Kansas City residents. Help provide sack lunches for Westport's homeless, hot meals at area shelters or participate in our food drives that have delivered over 75 tons of food to area pantries the last three years.
- Have a heart for the elderly? Join our members as we visit over 43 area nursing homes offering love and encouragement to residents.
- Interested in the Third World? Our teams provide medical care and build schools and churches on three continents.

So, if you want to make a real difference with your life, and you're not already part of an area church, we think you'll like how the Church of the Resurrection can help. Join us this weekend and see for yourself.

Relevant • Passionate • Life-Changing
The United Methodist Church of the Resurrection

The Church of the Resurrection
Sunday morning traditional worship 7:45, 9:00, 10:45 a.m.
Saturday and Sunday evening contemporary worship 5:00 p.m.
13720 Roe Avenue
Leawood, Kansas 66224
913.897.0120 • www.cor.org

While the focus of the postcard was on the series, the message was that here is a church that is helping people better understand Christianity and their faith. That understanding can make a difference in their lives.

We also use postcards to reach people with information about holiday worship and an invitation to join us. Because consistency of message helps awareness and memorability, our holiday postcards are basically lifted from our newspaper ads—but they take advantage of the additional space that a postcard provides to tell a more complete story of what Christmas at Resurrection is all about.

For example, recent postcard copy read as follows:

> We know that holiday traditions are important. Perhaps you host the holiday dinner or travel to the home of family or friends. Or, maybe it is trimming your tree and wrapping gifts while awaiting the joy of Christmas morning. This is a wonderful time of year.
>
> But Christmas is not complete without experiencing **candlelight Christmas Eve** in church.

If you don't have a church home, we would like to invite you to ours, where you'll hear **beautiful Christmas music**, old **familiar carols**, and the **retelling of the Christmas story** in a way that will touch your heart. We conclude each service with **the traditional passing of the lighted candles** as we sing "Silent Night."

Last year, our **seven candlelight services** were included in the USA Today list of ten great places to hear the Christmas gospel. This is one Christmas tradition you will not want to miss.

Website

There could be an entire ministry guide written on website design. However, for the purposes of this guide, I would simply like to comment on one aspect of website design: delivering your overall message.

A few years ago, our website was typical of so many sites out there. People arrived at our front page and it hit them with a bunch of information and links. But it never took the time to position the church or help explain how we wanted people to think about us.

Today, our front page is much simpler. It starts out with a single person and a testimonial that you can click on to read. And, the words "Relevant • Passionate • Life-Changing" rotate in a prominent position. The message is that we are about people whose lives are being changed. Information for links then follows.

I would like to encourage you to visit our site. We're located at **www.cor.org**. When you go there, consider whether you get a sense for who we are and what's important to us. I hope you do.

Communicating by E-mail

Let me close this section on message with comments on e-mail. Over time, we have collected over nine thousand e-mail addresses from our members and visitors. Each of them receives two e-mails from the church every week. This is not just a "members only" program because we recognize that our e-mails are also an outreach program that helps our visitors connect with the life of the church and understand how the life of the church is making a difference in people's lives.

General e-mail

▷ **The first e-mail** is our "Around the Corner," with its distinct logo. It is simply a news update on the programs and activities happening at the church. It provides our ministries with a way of com-

municating information about their programs and events on a weekly basis. Importantly, we keep the articles brief and provide links to additional information on our website. This allows *Around the Corner* to be a faster read and drives people to our website.

Pastor's enote

▷ **Our second email** is Senor Pastor Adam Hamilton's e-note. This is his opportunity to share with our church family (including members and visitors)

an enote from **Adam Hamilton**

what is on his heart and mind each week. It includes comment on the life of the church, thoughts on the coming sermon, and reflections on faith. It's addressed to the Resurrection Family.

Reinforcement

What I hope you will take away from this chapter is the importance of singlemindedly focusing on ONE MAIN IDEA and being sure that all of your communications reinforce that idea. I believe that one of the reasons we are successful at The Church of the Resurrection is that we have thought through our message and have worked to deliver that message with consistency.

CHAPTER FOUR

Empowering Your Members

Not long ago, I was at a meeting of communications directors from large churches. A number of them worked at churches with more than twenty thousand members and a track record of success in attracting unchurched people to their doors. I was excited about this opportunity because I hoped I could get an answer to my number one question. It may be a question that you have asked (or asked yourself) more than once. How do I know that what I am doing is working? Or put another way, How do I measure success? If you have asked this question, you'll be interested to know that everyone in the room basically had the same answer. "Good question. I don't know."

Now there's a scary thought. Here were what I considered to be the experts in the field of church communications. Talented people who spend large amounts of money every year planning and executing programs designed to reach out to those with little or no faith and convince them that they should be attending church. And they had no idea whether those programs were working other than their worship attendance was growing.

How Do You Measure Response?

I shouldn't have been surprised by the answer. I know that measuring the results of an advertising or marketing program is difficult unless you have a specific offer or a coupon so you can measure response. And I have yet to hear of a church that has used coupons redeemable at the door to the sanctuary. The old adage among advertisers is that "I know that half of my advertising dollars are wasted, but I don't know which half."

In fact, one way that we do try to figure out which of our marketing and advertising programs is working best is to ask our new members what first brought them to our church. While I would like to hear them say, "Oh, it was a postcard I received" or "I saw a newspaper ad," the reality is that over 90 percent of our new members tell us it was a personal invitation from a neighbor, fellow worker, or relative. So you have to wonder, if personal invitation is the key to bringing first-time visitors to the church, why do we spend money on advertising and mail programs? I like to think that our answer to that question makes some sense.

Marketing Bolsters Personal Invitation

At Resurrection, we believe that our marketing and advertising efforts lay a foundation of awareness that makes extending a personal invitation easier and a positive response to that invitation more likely. We believe that our members will be more likely to ask someone to join them for weekend worship if the person they are inviting knows something about our church. And, we believe that a person is more likely to say yes to that invitation if they are already somewhat familiar with the church. So, in effect, our marketing and advertising efforts help empower our members to invite someone they know who doesn't have a church home.

Postcards

We even take this empowering idea a step further. Every time we send out a postcard, the weekend before it is mailed, we put one in every worship bulletin. We don't do this just so our members can see what we are sending. Pastor Adam Hamilton calls attention to the postcard and encourages our members to take it home, put it in the hands of someone who needs to see it, and invite him or her to worship. The postcard then simply makes extending an invitation easier for our members.

Business cards

Here's one more idea to make extending an invitation easy. We have business cards with our worship times, our location, our phone number, and our web address available at our Information Center. Members can pick them up and give them to people they'd like to see join them for worship. Last spring, we printed over thirty thousand of these cards and they didn't cost us a dime. When we printed our postcards for Easter, we added the business cards to the extra space on the sheet on which the postcards were being printed. You can do the same the next time you are printing something if you plan ahead.

Using the web

We've also learned to use our website to empower our members. Prior to the holidays or a sermon series

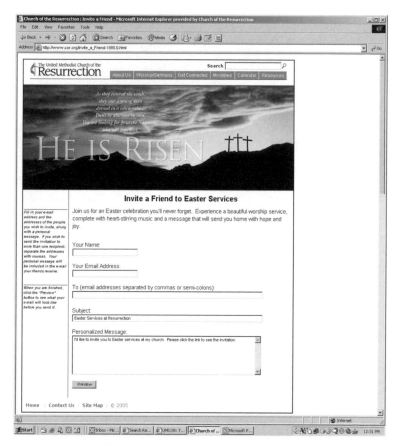

that should be particularly relevant to our target audience, our members can go online and send an e-vite—an e-mail invitation—to someone they may know who is in need of a church home. The e-vite is formatted so that all they have to do is enter their name and the e-mail address of the person they'd like to send it to, or they can enhance it with a personal note. We make it as easy as possible for our members to get over that hurdle of inviting someone to church. Above is an illustration of our e-vite form used one year for Easter.

I have heard of a number of research studies asking people who hadn't been attending church what motivated them to give church a try. Like our own new members, the answer for at least 80 percent of those surveyed is consistently **personal invitation**. Ask yourself how you can empower your members to extend that invitation. This may be the most effective means of bringing those in your community to your front door on Sunday morning.

When you make a concerted effort to attract visitors, be sure that your members know to expect those visitors when they show up on Sunday. We do it by placing our postcards in the bulletins and talking about all the visitors we anticipate will join us for holiday worship. The point is that you want your members to be on the lookout for visitors and to welcome them.

CHAPTER FIVE

Getting Everything Done

By now some pretty good ideas that you would be interested in developing are materializing, but the question becomes, "How am I going to get these things done?" You have basically four options: do it yourself, talented volunteers, freelancers, advertising agency.

Whether you are doing it yourself or working with volunteers, freelancers, or an agency, remember to stay strategic. Start with a clear understanding of who you are as a church; define who you are trying to reach and what message you want to communicate to them. Then you can think about the details of what is the best way to reach that audience both through media selection and creative execution.

While I can't guarantee that this approach will lead to unqualified success in bringing new people to your front doors, I do believe that it will enable you to develop more effective communications to those in your community who are in need of your message and your ministry.

Options

Unfortunately, there isn't a website that I can send you to where they sell magic wands. At least not that I know of—and I've looked. However, you do have a choice of several options.

Do it yourself

▷ **The first option** is to do it yourself. Perhaps you have some creative talent hidden away in the recesses of your mind. You can write some copy or you know something about desktop publishing. Start slow, think strategically, but try some things and see what develops. You may discover that you enjoy creating advertising and communications pieces—and that you are pretty good at it.

Importantly, doing it yourself doesn't mean doing it alone. Bounce your ideas off others just to check and see if the direction you are headed is a good one. In fact, whether you are doing it yourself or using one of the other development options, it's a good idea to keep the senior pastor, or whoever else will be involved in approving what you plan to do, in the loop. Have this person check off at the concept stage and after copy development. This will avoid surprises and ensure that you aren't doing a lot of work on an idea that others don't agree with. Nothing is worse than having to start over at square one.

Here is another idea that can help you feel like you have a support group. Recently in Kansas City, we formed a group of people who are responsible for their church's communications. We have large, medium, and even small churches included and meet monthly to talk about what we do. Our discussions range from working with the media, developing stewardship campaigns, creating effective websites, and following up with first-time visitors to simply getting things done in Kansas City. It is a great forum and provides us with a chance to share ideas and learning. It's not that hard to get a group started—you can probably do the same in your town or area. It is well worth the effort.

Talented volunteers

▷ **The second option**. Perhaps creating mailers and ads or writing a radio script may simply not be in your skill set. Let's say you don't have the time or the confidence required to go it on your own. If that is the case, you may want to go the volunteer route. That may sound pretty good, but you wonder how you go about finding the volunteers with the right talents and know-how.

Start by simply putting out the word that you are looking for help. Use your bulletin, newsletter, e-mail or other internal forms of communications that reach your congregation to say that you are looking for people with a background in advertising, marketing, design, writing, or media relations to help with church communications. See who responds. Then if you still think you need more or different talents, ask those folks for names of people they know who might be able and interested in helping. Creative people tend to know other creative people, and your initial volunteers may actually help you recruit.

Keep in mind, you don't need a large number of people. Some of our best volunteer work is done by a two-person team. But they are very talented, work well together, and have a passion for helping God's church succeed. Also, both are long-time members of Resurrection and, as a result, have a good sense for our tone or voice and our language. This understanding simply increases their success and reduces our development time on projects. If you put togeth-er a list of all that you would like to see a creative team develop, it probably is a short enough list that a small team can get the job done.

Once you have a team on board, really take advantage of the individuals' expertise and fresh perspective. Give them ownership of your marketing. Solicit their ideas from the beginning and find ways that each member can contribute. From experience, I know that one thing that creative people don't like is being micromanaged. You need to give them a free hand and then see what happens. When I do this, I am consistently amazed by how creative people exceed my expectations. They have a way of thinking about things, looking at things, and expressing ideas that most of us just don't have. It is exciting to watch them work.

That doesn't mean that you can pass out the assignment and then sit back and wait for the finished work. You will need to engage the team in discussions about strategies, the tactics that will deliver on those strategies, and budgets and timetables. Play the role of project manager. Stay close enough to your volunteers while they work to ensure that they are staying on track. I've worked with many great volunteers, but I have also worked with a few who dropped the ball. They got busy with other things and didn't follow through as I had hoped or expected. Staying close and setting deadlines won't guarantee that this won't happen, but it helps.

Freelancers

▷ **Option number three** is that you can hire someone to do the job for you. This could be a freelance writer or designer or both. This person may even be a member of your congregation. Freelancers work independently on a project basis, frequently out of their home, and typically are less expensive than hiring an advertising agency. That doesn't mean that a freelancer is less talented. The ones that I have worked with are very good. They just like being independent.

If you hire a freelancer to help with your marketing, you should still work with him or her in the same ways mentioned as volunteers. However, you will have to pay the freelancer, either on an hourly basis or, better still, offer to pay on a project basis—for a particular job. Using this form of up-front agreement with the freelancer minimizes the bookkeeping and the worry about how many hours the freelancer is working against a project.

Whether you work with freelancers or volunteers, it is important that you honor their time and their schedules. Just because they aren't keeping office hours doesn't mean that they are available on evenings and weekends. Talk with them about how they like to work and when the best times to meet are. I know this will be appreciated.

Also, ask yourself how you can help volunteers or freelancers work more efficiently and effectively. What do they need from you to make effective use of their time? The better prepared you are with knowing what you want to accomplish, the better they can work toward that goal.

Advertising agency

▷ **The fourth option** is to hire an advertising agency. Agencies, whether they are large, medium, or even small, can do a wide range of things for you. They can develop a marketing plan. They can create print ads, radio and television commercials, mail pieces, websites, banners, or posters. They can buy media and give you advice on the best ways to reach your target.

POTENTIAL PITFALL

However, the more that advertising agencies do for you, the more they are going to charge you. So, if you go this route, be selective. Figure out what things you can do yourself and where you really need the help. Be specific in what you expect from the advertising agency and the amount of money you can spend. With proper management, advertising costs can be kept under control.

The challenge to hiring an advertising agency, or a freelancer for that matter, is finding the right one. In all likelihood, the ones you consider will not have worked for a church before. So how do you choose? I would recommend that you meet with them and review the work that they have done for other clients. If you are developing a print campaign, look for those with expertise in print and whose work you like. If you are planning a radio campaign, look for those who have done a lot of work in radio. When you meet with them, be sure to discuss their fee structure and, importantly, spend some time just getting to know them. I look for people with a good Christian heart, an understanding of our values as a church, and an interest in the project. I realize that there will be more of a learning curve because they are going to have to learn our style and voice, but agencies and freelancers are used to learning new businesses.

Sometimes advertising agencies will work for a not-for-profit organization without charge—on a pro bono basis. Most often there are two reasons an agency will accept a pro bono client. First, it's a way of giving back to the community. Contributing their talents and expertise to groups like the scouting program or community theater is their way of being good citizens. Second, they may see it as an opportunity to do some fresh and interesting work. For creative people, nothing is worse than getting into a rut. And doing something for a not-for-profit may give them the chance to do something that is different from the work they do for their paying clients. There's no guarantee that an agency will work for your church pro bono, but it doesn't hurt to ask.

Conclusions

Okay. It's time to get to work. Hopefully this ministry guide has provided you with enough strategies, concepts, and ideas to get you started. As you do, here are what I think are the most important things to keep in mind.

▷ **Always** think strategically. Define who you want to reach with your message and then tailor your message to speak directly to them. Spend the time to develop your message strategy and then use it as your roadmap for everything. Consistently ask yourself during the development process whether you are communicating your message clearly and in ways that will resonate with your target audience. Your message strategy will also be the final test for whether you are communicating what you meant to say.

▷ **Stay** single-minded in your message. Everything you do should fit under the umbrella of your message strategy, whether it is a television commercial, a print ad, a mail piece or even a poster or flyer. If your materials look and sound different from each other, it's likely your message will get lost in the confusion.

▷ **Do** only what you can do well and what you can afford to do well. In many cases, your communications will be your church's first introduction to your target. Make sure it is a good first impression. Don't settle for second best. Instead, make sure that everything you do is work that you are proud of. In fact, that's actually pretty good advice for life in general.

▷ **Remember** that personal invitation will always be the most effective means of attracting first-time visitors. So, be sure that you are empowering your members to extend that personal invitation by encouraging it and putting materials in their hands to make it easy for them to do.

▷ **Begin** each project by asking God to help you reach those in your community who need what your church can offer. Don't try to do it all by yourself. Put the project in God's hands and promise to do all that you are able to do to deliver God's message. God makes a great partner. I never did this when I worked in the secular world, and it has been the greatest lesson of my life. Now, when I start a project that seems overwhelming in terms of what has to be done and with difficult deadlines, I start with prayer. Turning the project over to God takes the weight off of my shoulders and enables me to work without feeling pressure. Every time I have done this, things just seem to work out.